flag eti
& visual s

G000123676

Written by the RYA and
Commander R L Hewitt MVO RN

First Published (1969) as Flags
and Signals.

Revised into an RYA book 1975.

Reprinted June 1987 and 1989.

This edition updated October 2001.

An RYA publication

Published by
The Royal Yachting Association
RYA House Romsey Road Eastleigh
Hampshire SO50 9YA
Tel: +44 (0)23 8062 7400
Fax: +44 (0)23 8062 9924
Email: admin@rya.org.uk
Web: www.rya.org.uk

CONTENTS

FOREWORD

Flag etiquette, as a whole, is a mixture of law and good manners which have risen out of tradition. The second point is important as bad manners can offend and upset others. It is good, therefore, to make the effort to understand and observe the traditions and customs of motor or sail cruising. This book aims to clarify the main points of flag etiquette and other visual signalling methods. Flag etiquette is not difficult, the basic rules are simple and the satisfaction gained from doing it right should not be underestimated.

Acknowledgement must be given to those people who have helped the RYA to produce this book over its various editions. These are the late Major Heckstall-Smith, one time editor of *Yachting World* and Captain EMC Barraclough CBE RN (retd). Although this book contains a great deal of additional material which will be useful to sailors, the compilers of the first edition leaned heavily on Captain Barraclough's book entitled *Yacht Flags and Ensigns,* later re-titled *Flag Etiquette for Yachts*.

We hope you enjoy this book and gain the satisfaction of knowing that your flag etiquette is spot on.

Flags worn by and flown from British yachts

The flags and Ensigns customarily worn by and flown from British yachts comprise:

1. The Ensign.
2. The club burgee or special flag of officers of a yacht club.
3. House flags.
4. Special flags.
5. Racing flags occasionally.
6. Prize flags.

The history of the use of Ensigns dates right back to about 1570. In those days, the Ensigns almost invariably had the St George's Cross in the canton where the Union Flag is in the present Ensign. The remainder of the Ensign's area was covered with horizontal stripes indicating the port from which the vessel hailed. The use of such Ensigns declined and early in the seventeenth century the Red, White and Blue Ensigns began to be used. In 1674 the Red Ensign became the Ensign of British merchant ships.

Yacht clubs started being formed somewhere round about 1720, and it is believed that the Royal Cork Yacht Club, originally called the Water Club of the Harbour of Cork, was the first. It was reformed in 1822 as the Cork Yacht Club.

The Cumberland Society was formed by the Duke of Cumberland in 1775 and in 1823 became the Thames Yacht Club. The prefix 'Royal' was granted in 1830 and on 19 February 1835 the club was granted an Admiralty Warrant to wear a plain White Ensign bearing in the fly a crown over the letters RTYC in red. Prior to, and after that date, a number of clubs were happily wearing Ensigns without authority. The records show that the Royal Yacht Squadron was granted the right to wear the White Ensign in 1829 but, at that date, the Red Ensign was still the senior Ensign.

In 1859 the Admiralty withdrew all Warrants to wear the White Ensign still existing except from the Royal Yacht Squadron. The right to wear the Blue Ensign is dealt with later in this book.

THE ENSIGN

Generally, the use of the national Ensign is governed by statutes and statutory regulations (The Merchant Shipping Acts and Queen's Regulations for the Royal Navy), although in part it is governed by custom and tradition except that the design and manner of use of these flags must not conflict with any existing regulation or recognised signal code.

The Ensign is the national flag and denotes the country of registration. Generally this will follow the nationality of the owner, although Spain for example, has rules for the registration in Spain of yachts owned by resident foreigners. Individuals affected by such rules would be required to fly the Spanish ensign, being the flag of the country of registration rather than that of the owner's nationality.

Times during which Ensigns should be worn

At sea

The rules for peacetime are set out in full, although it is obviously unlikely that a yacht will find itself in the situation described in subsection 1 below:

1. The Ensign should be worn continuously at sea by day and by night by a vessel flying or escorting a Royal Standard or Flag of a Head of State.

2. The Ensign is to be hoisted *if there is sufficient light for it to be seen, upon passing or meeting one of Her Majesty's Ships, and also, unless there should be some reason to the contrary, on falling in with any other ship or ships at sea, or when within sight of or near to land, and especially when passing or*

approaching forts, batteries, signal or coast guard stations, lighthouses or towns. This is the strict rule and appears to pre-suppose that there is no objection to hauling the Ensign down during darkness or when out of sight of land or other ships.

3. When racing, the RORC lay down the rule that an Ensign should not be worn after the five minute gun, and during a race (unless the yacht has retired) and should be worn after the yacht has crossed the finishing line.

4. It used to be accepted procedure at most regattas for yachts larger than dinghies to leave their moorings wearing an Ensign but this practice has virtually ceased. However, if the Ensign is worn, it and its staff should be removed before or at the five minute gun to signify that the yacht is subject to ISAF rules.

In harbour

In British waters, the proper time for hoisting the Ensign is 0800 (0900 in the winter months between 1 November and 14 February inclusive). Ensigns are always lowered at sunset or at 2100 local time, if earlier.

When abroad, the local custom should be followed; generally this will be found to be the same as in British waters, although, in most places with a temperate climate, colours are hoisted at 0800 throughout the year, while in extreme northern and southern latitudes, when sunrise is later than 0900 colours are made at sunrise.

Similarly, during the summer months in high latitudes, when sunset may not occur until a very late hour, it is customary to fix an arbitrary time (normally 2100) for lowering the colours.

Yachts should take their time for hoisting and lowering colours from the senior ship present. If ships of the Royal Navy are present, the ship of the senior naval officer is the senior ship present; if none of HM ships are present, the principal yacht club in the port should give the time by hoisting and lowering the Ensign at its flag staff, and on ceremonial occasions by a signal such as the firing of a gun.

Failing either of the above, yachts should endeavour to follow the actions of the senior flag officer of a yacht club, if one is present. The flag officers of clubs should appreciate that they have this responsibility.

As will be seen in the Conditions about the wearing of special Ensigns (page 10 para 7) a *special* Ensign can only be worn when the owner is in *effective control* of the yacht. If the holder of the permit is absent from the port such a yacht can only wear the Red Ensign.

The crew (paid or unpaid) should therefore hoist the Red Ensign at 0800 (0900 in winter). If, during the day, the owner who holds a permit to wear a special Ensign comes aboard then the Red Ensign may be replaced with the Ensign to which he is entitled. Similarly, if he leaves the yacht not intending to remain in the port, then the Red Ensign should be substituted for the special ensign .

Clearly the circumstances of the use of most yachts preclude strict compliance with the timing of hoisting Ensigns. It is accepted that as soon as the crew join the yacht within the prescribed hours then the correct Ensign will be hoisted.

Ashore

The White and Blue Ensigns of Her Majesty's Fleet are purely maritime flags and in general their use on shore is incorrect. There has, however, been a customary extension of the use of the White Ensign (from the harbour ship used as a Fleet establishment) to barracks and other buildings on shore serving the same purpose. There has been a parallel extension of the use of these from yachts, Customs vessels and the like, to their headquarters on the coast - the club house or Customs office.

It is common also for the White and Blue Ensigns to be used on cenotaphs and other memorials to naval personnel.

As the flying of Ensigns and burgees from the club houses of yacht clubs is recognised, it is desirable to give some guidance on this point.

Generally, it can be assumed that yacht and sailing clubs should proceed exactly as if they were *registered British ships*. In other words, a yacht club should wear the Ensign of the club on the gaff of its flagstaff and its burgee - or the special flag of the senior officer of the club present in the port - at the flagstaff head.

The same rules for *dressing ship* apply. The flags should be hoisted at the time of making colours in the morning and lowered at sunset.

With these exceptions, the use of Ensigns ashore is incorrect.

If a club wishes to extend a particular courtesy to another club, where, for example, members are visiting for the purpose of a team race, then the burgee of the visiting club may be flown at the starboard yard-arm. If this club is an overseas club, then its national maritime Ensign should be flown at the starboard yard-arm and the burgee flown from the port yard-arm.

Positions from which to wear Ensigns

In general, the guiding rule is that the most important flag should be most prominently displayed and in the most important position, the second most important flag in the second most important position. and so on. Dating from the time of sailing ships, the after part of the ship has been considered the most important part, as the officers were accommodated aft and the ship conned and worked from the poop and quarter-deck.

The Ensign of the country to which the yacht belongs is the most important of the flags and it should be worn in the after part of the ship and most prominently displayed, usually from its own special staff on the taffrail.

It is, however, impossible for some ships to keep the Ensign staff shipped when under way owing to interference by sails or gear. When this occurs, the Ensign should be worn in a position as near as possible to that which it would occupy when flying from its staff.

In gaff-rigged ships this is the peak of the sail on the after mast (i.e. mainsail of single-masted vessels and schooners, and the mizzen of three-masted vessels, yawls and ketches).

This position has been in use so long that it can be laid down that a gaff-rigged yacht when at sea may wear her Ensign either at the peak or at the Ensign staff, whichever is preferred.

Bermudan-rigged yachts present a difficulty; in the past some have worn their Ensigns from a position approximately two-thirds up the leech of the after sail, but this position is unsatisfactory because the Ensign may sometimes curl into the lee of the sail and does not fly out and, unless a yacht has no other position from which to wear the Ensign, is not recommended.

Bermudan-rigged yachts when at sea should wear the Ensign as follows:

1. For all types: whenever possible from the Ensign staff on the taffrail.

2. For single-masted yachts, schooners, or ships with more than two masts in which the after-mast is as tall as, or taller than, the other masts and the Ensign staff cannot be used, there is no alternative but to wear the Ensign in a position two-thirds up the leech of the after sail.

3. For yawls, ketches and yachts with more than two masts where the after mast is shorter than the mainmast, then the Ensign may be worn at a staff at the mizzen masthead.

In power-driven yachts which have an after-mast fitted with a gaff, the Ensign may be worn at the peak of this gaff when at sea.

The Red Ensign

This is the particular national flag of the British merchantman and as yachts are classed as merchantmen, they are entitled to wear the Ensign under the terms of the Merchant Shipping Acts.

By the same Acts, a vessel over 50 tons gross is compelled to wear her colours when entering or leaving a British port and all vessels (unless registered as fishing vessels) must wear their proper national colours when entering or leaving a foreign port.

A *registered yacht* is entitled and required to wear the Red Ensign, and for an unregistered yacht it can be assumed that although not *entitled*, she can and should wear the Red Ensign on all occasions when it is proper to show the national colours.

The Red Ensign should be carried on board even if not worn.

The special Ensigns

Certain yacht clubs (listed in the Navy list) are granted the privilege of using a special Ensign and members of such a club may wear that Ensign on their yachts provided they comply with the conditions of a Warrant issued before 1 April 1985 or the conditions of a permit issued to them by the Secretary of the club after that date. The latter Conditions are set out in full on pages 12 to 15.

The special Ensigns are:

The White Ensign of Her Majesty's Fleet which is used exclusively by the Royal Yacht Squadron.

The Blue Ensign (undefaced) and the Blue or Red Ensign with the badge, emblem or crest of a particular yacht club in the fly.

The privilege of wearing these is granted by the Secretary of State for Defence on behalf of HM The Queen. Any yacht club granted this privilege is usually of some antiquity and must fulfil other conditions including having in its members' ownership a considerable tonnage of cruising sea-going vessels. Nowadays the list of such privileged clubs is seldom expanded.

It is worth making a few points other than the notes by the RYA contained in the official conditions.

A privileged owner has no right to wear the yacht's Ensign elsewhere than on board that yacht.

A special Ensign should never be worn without the burgee of the entitled club or a Flag Officer's flag of that club.

Conditions governing the issue of yacht permits to members of entitled yacht clubs in the United Kingdom and Channel Islands

In Section 73 of the Merchant Shipping Act 1894, it is an offence to hoist on board any ship or boat belonging to any British subject certain colours, flags and pendants without a Warrant from Her Majesty the Queen or from the Secretary of State for Defence.

The maximum penalty is one thousand pounds for each offence. Among the prohibited flags are the Union Flag, The White Ensign, the Blue Ensign (plain or defaced) and the Red Ensign with any defacement.

The prohibition applies to any ship or boat belonging to any British subject wherever it may be, and so extends not only to tidal waters but equally to rivers, lakes and inland waters generally.

Yachts may not wear the special Ensigns prohibited above except:

(a) Under a Warrant issued to the yacht owner by the Secretary of State for Defence prior to 1 April 1985 and in accordance with the conditions stated thereon.

(b) Under a permit issued to the yacht owner by a yacht club from 1 April 1985 onwards and in accordance with the Conditions set out below.

RYA note

As will be seen undefaced Union Flag is never flown by merchant ships or yachts.

The term *yacht* used above may of course include both sailing and motor yachts.

Conditions

1. permit

The yacht must be issued with a permit by a yacht club pursuant to the granting of a Warrant to that club by the Secretary of State for Defence.

The validity period of the permit is left to the discretion of the individual yacht club.

2. Registration and measurement

(a) Registration. The yacht must be a ship registered under either:

 (1) Part 1 of the Merchant Shipping Act 1894; (Part 1 Registration)

 (2) The Merchant Shipping Act 1983. (Small Ships Register SSR)

(b) Measurement. The yacht must measure not less than:

 (1) Two tons gross if registered under (a)(1) above

 (2) Seven metres in length overall if registered under (a)(2) above.

RYA note

Yachts entitled to be registered on the Small Ships Register are measured by length rather than by tonnage.

Those below seven metres length overall on that Register do not qualify to wear a special Ensign

3. Membership of designated yacht club

The owner or owners of the yacht must have current membership of one of the yacht clubs in the United Kingdom or Channel Islands to which a Warrant has been issued and which is designated in the Navy List.

RYA note

Yacht Warrants are, under this scheme, issued to each entitled yacht club and authorise the flag Officers and Committee to issue permits to members whose yachts satisfy the qualifying conditions.

4. Nationality

The owner or owners must be British subjects.

5. Use of yacht

(a) The special Ensign may only be worn on a yacht used exclusively for private and personal purposes of the yachtsman to whom the permit is issued.

(b) The yacht must not be used for any professional, business or commercial purpose. A yacht whose name incorporates a name, product or trademark used for business or commercial purposes is not eligible for a permit.

(c) A yacht which is never used for cruising (eg a houseboat) is ineligible for a permit.

RYA note

Cruising, of course, includes a sea-going *racing* yacht.

6. Limited companies

A yacht which is the property of a limited Company may be eligible for a permit provided the provisions of Condition 5 are complied with and the user is a British subject and a member of a designated yacht club.

RYA note

Yachts owned by limited companies are not eligible to be registered on the Small Ships Register hence such yachts must be registered under the procedure for registration contained in Part I of the Merchant Shipping Act 1894 (See Condition 2).

7. Presence of holder of permit

Except under the provisions of Condition 6, a permit does not confer any authority while the yacht is being sailed by anyone other than the owner in person.

Thus a special Ensign may not be worn unless the owner or user (see Condition 6) of the yacht is on board, or in effective, in control of her when she is in harbour or at anchor near the shore, and the club's burgee is flown at the main masthead, or other suitable position.

The permit must always be carried on board when a special Ensign is worn.

RYA note

The first sentence of this Condition may tend to confuse! But the Condition read as a whole makes it clear that, provided the owner is on board, any member of the crew may physically sail the yacht whilst the special Ensign is being worn.

8. Separate authorisation from each club

If the owner or user belongs to more than one of the designated clubs, he must have on board the permit authorising the particular Ensign which is being worn.

9. Charter or loan of yacht for which a permit has been issued.

When a yacht for which a permit has been issued to a member of a designated yacht club is occasionally and for a short period let out on charter such action will not be held to infringe Condition 5 and will not lead to permanent disqualification. However, the permit must be withdrawn by the Secretary of the yacht club.

Application may be made for a fresh permit on termination of the period of charter.

RYA note

A yacht which is chartered out to a person who is not a member of a designated club is not entitled to wear the special Ensign of an entitled club. Properly, such a yacht if chartered to a British subject would wear the Red Ensign.

10 .Return of permit

When a yacht is sold or there is a change of ownership or the owner ceases to be a member of the club, the permit must at once be surrendered to the Secretary of the club who shall forthwith cancel it.

11. Alterations to permits

No alterations are to be made to permits.

If the name of the yacht is changed, or alterations are made which affect the register, the permit is to be withdrawn by the Secretary of the club.

A new permit may be issued provided these conditions are otherwise satisfied.

12. Permits lost or stolen

In the event of a permit being lost or stolen, the member must forward to the Secretary of the club a report on the circumstances of the loss and the steps taken to recover it. The secretary may, at his discretion, issue a fresh permit.

13. Tenders

The special Ensign may be worn by any boat which belongs to the yacht and can conveniently be hoisted on board her.

14. Foreign cruises

When cruising in foreign waters, a yacht for which a permit to wear a special Ensign has been issued should take care to avoid any action which might result in complications with a foreign power.

To this end, members intending to visit foreign waters affected by war or serious disturbances must give particulars of their voyage to the Secretary of the club, who should immediately inform the Ministry of Defence (Naval Law Division), Whitehall, London SW1A 2HB.

15. Breach of conditions

A permit for a yacht to wear a special Ensign becomes invalid if the provisions of the above Conditions are not met.

16. Etiquette

permit holders may wish to comply with the custom, when in harbour, of hoisting the Ensign at 0800 (0900 between 1 November and 14 February) and lowering the Ensign at sunset (or 2100 local time if earlier).

RYA note

This condition is a gentle reminder to observe the customs and traditions of honouring the Colours and will no doubt meet with the approval of all those who have gone to the trouble to obtain a permit to wear a *special* Ensign. Equally, it would be appropriate to remind readers that all Ensigns should be in a presentable condition. The RYA has heard in the past of yachts being arrested in foreign waters because courtesy Ensigns were in an unsavoury condition!

Foreign or courtesy Ensigns

It is customary, but not obligatory, when lying in a foreign port, to fly the maritime Ensign of the country being visited, as a mark of courtesy. The courtesy Ensign is usually considerably smaller than the vessel's Ensign and it would appear to be custom for it to be struck at the same time as the yacht's own Ensign, although opinions differ on this point.

The Ensign should, in the case of a single-masted vessel, be flown at the starboard topsail yard, or upper crosstrees. In the case of yachts with more than one mast it may be flown either at this position or at the fore or mizzen masthead. But, whenever it is flown, care should be taken that it is not hoisted at a position inferior to any other flag except the yacht's own national Ensign and club burgee or, in the case of a yacht club's flag officer, the flag officer's personal flag.

The British maritime Ensign for use as a courtesy Ensign is the Red Ensign and not the Union Flag.

CLUB BURGEES AND FLAGS OF FLAG OFFICERS

Club burgee

Each yacht or sailing club has its own burgee and in Great Britain this is a triangular flag. Yacht clubs are free to choose their own design of burgee so long as it does not contravene any Ministry regulation or can be confused with any other flag, Ensign or burgee. A new club should make every investigation to see that the burgee proposed conforms with the regulations and is not too similar to an already existing burgee design.

Flag Officer's flags

Most yacht clubs authorise a special flag to be used by the flag officers of the club. Customarily the design of these flags is generally the same as the club burgee. A Commodore flies a broad (or swallow-tailed) pendant. The Vice and Rear Commodore's pendants are distinguished from the Commodore's pendant by one and two balls respectively in the cantons next to the hoist. (See example on inside back cover).

Special flag of past Commodore, Vice-President, Admiral etc.

Although there is no naval custom to follow in this respect, it is quite usual for past Commodores and others to fly, at the masthead, a rectangular flag, similar to the club burgee in design and bearing the club's badge, emblem or crest.

General

It goes without saying that the owner of a yacht should only fly the burgees of yacht clubs of which he is a member.

A person who has chartered or been lent a yacht should use the burgees of yacht clubs of which he is a member, and not the burgees of yacht clubs of which the absent owner is a member.

Traditionally a yacht normally displays only one burgee.

The custom of flying one burgee at the truck and the burgee of another club at the starboard crosstrees is not strictly correct. The etiquette as to which burgee should be flown when the owner is a member of more than one club is explained under the heading Membership of more than one club on page 13.

The yacht club burgee should be flown with the correct Ensign, and the Ensign may be either the special Ensign of the club whose burgee is being flown, or an undefaced Red Ensign. The burgee may, however, be flown on its own in a small boat which would not normally wear an Ensign, or in a larger yacht at sea which may strike its Ensign when away from land or other ships.

Many yacht owners, when in harbour at night, will strike both their Ensign and their burgee whilst in harbour, and these will be lowered at sunset or at 2100, whichever is earlier, or when the owner goes ashore if it is before this time.

Some yachtsmen nowadays, however, strike only the Ensign and leave the club burgee flying during the hours of darkness during such time as the owner is in the vicinity of the yacht and can be described as being in effective control of the yacht.

The special flag of a Flag Officer of a yacht club corresponds in principle to the personal or distinguishing flag of a Flag Officer in Her Majesty's Fleet. In the Royal Navy, this flag is flown continuously by day and by night whilst the Flag Officer is in exercise of his command. Thus the special flag of a Flag Officer of a yacht club should be flown continuously by day and by night, whenever the owner is in the vicinity of the yacht and can be described as being *in effective control* of his yacht, except when he chooses to fly a racing flag or is required by the sailing instructions so to do. As with the Ensign, when at sea, there is no objection to hauling the flag down during the hours of darkness or when out of sight of land or other ships.

Position of burgee or Flag Officer's flag

Both these flags should be flown from a staff at the main masthead. The starboard crosstree is considered a reasonable alternative for racing yachts with no masthead halyard, or with too many instruments at the masthead. A gaff rigged cutter carrying a big jackyard topsail may fly the burgee or Flag Officer's special flag from the end of the topsail yard.

In powerboats which have no mast the burgee may be flown from a staff on the bow or over the wheelhouse.

Membership of more than one club

Although it will usually be obvious which burgee or Flag Officer's flag should be flown the following rules are suggested for guidance:

1. If an owner is a Flag Officer of a yacht club he should generally fly his Flag Officer's flag and wear the appropriate Ensign in preference to any other burgee and Ensign, wherever he may be.

2. If an owner is not a Flag Officer but is a member of a yacht club in the port in which his yacht is lying then he should use the Ensign and burgee of that club.

3. If an owner belongs to several clubs in one port, then the Ensign and burgee of

the senior club should normally be used, except on the occasions when another club in the port is having a regatta or some such function, when the Ensign and burgee of that club should be used.

It is also traditional that where a yacht is engaged in some function organised by one of the owner's clubs, then it is in order for the Ensign and burgee of that club to be used. For example, the RORC Ensign and burgee would be worn by yachts which are assembling for the start of a race organised by that club. Where a club is entitled to a special Ensign, members should fly the appropriate club burgee or Flag Officer's flag with that special Ensign.

4. In certain clubs, such as the Service Clubs, Royal Cruising Club, Royal Ocean Racing Club and Little Ship Club (which are national clubs and have no local affiliations), it is correct for an owner to use the Ensign and burgee of any of these clubs of which he is a member whenever his yacht is in a place where there is no yacht club of which he is a member.

HOUSE FLAGS
Euro flag

The dark blue European Union flag with twelve gold mullets (stars, single point uppermost). This is not an Ensign and may not be defaced with the Union flag. It is a house flag and should be accorded the same procedures and positioning as other house flags.

RYA flag

A square flag hoisted in harbour at the crosstrees (starboard yard-arm or rigging) by members of the Royal Yachting Association, the National Authority and governing body protecting the interests of yachtsmen.

It is a white square flag with a broad blue cross defaced in the centre with a diamond laid horizontal in red colour, representing yachts under various points of sailing.

The owner's house flag or distinguishing flag

All shipping companies have a private flag which, when flown from a ship, denotes the company to which the vessel belongs. In the same way, an individual owner of a yacht may use his own distinguishing or house flag. The use of this flag is optional, and the design is a matter entirely for the owner, the only stipulation being that the design must not conflict with an existing regulation or any other existing Ensign, flag or burgee. It is none too easy to establish that this design does not conflict with other designs. At present there is no publication which indicates all designs, even if they had all been scrutinised.

The owner of a yacht, or a person who has chartered or been lent a yacht, may use his personal house flag in his own yacht or in one he has chartered or been lent.

House flags may be flown with or without an Ensign but are never flown in vessels wearing the White Ensign.

If any owner wishes to use his own house flag, it should be hoisted and lowered at the same time as the club burgee or the special flag of a Flag Officer of a yacht club. Customarily, the owner's house flag is only flown when the owner is actually on board his yacht.

In single-masted yachts, the house flag should be flown from the starboard yard-arm or, if there is no yard-arm, from the starboard upper crosstrees or similar position.

In schooners or yachts with more than two masts, it should be flown from the fore masthead.

In yawls or ketches, it may be flown from the mizzen masthead or from the yard-arm or crosstrees of the mainmast.

It is perhaps worth pointing out that the flying of house flags from this position whilst at sea could be confusing since signals would be flown from the same position.

In recent years, the large racing yachts have established a new type of *House Flag*, normally flown in the forepart of the vessel in marinas when regattas are in progress. The flag is extremely large and bears what may be described as personally designed armorial designs.

The European Union flag is a house flag and should only be flown as such. The 12 stars (or mullets) should have the single point upwards and the flag may not include a Union Flag.

CHARTERED VESSELS

Leaving aside the question of the right to wear a special Ensign we should, perhaps, discuss the situation where a yachtsman charters the yacht of another.

Clearly, the yacht cannot change nationality. Hence, if a British subject charters a German yacht it should wear German colours. In the case of a charter by one British subject from another British subject there is no problem. The Red Ensign will suffice.

Clearly, the courtesy Ensign of the country being visited should be worn at the starboard crosstrees.

The burgee should be of a club to which the charterer belongs.

The practice has sprung up of the charterer indicating his own nationality, if it is different from the yacht's, by wearing a small courtesy Ensign or maritime flag at the port crosstrees.

SPECIAL FLAGS
The Union Flag

The Union Flag, except as stated below, is flown only by ships of the Royal Navy and HM Air Force vessels, and never by merchant ships or yachts.

The Union Flag, generally defaced by a badge in the centre, is the official flag of certain high officers of the Government, such as governors of colonies. If one of these officers is embarked in an official capacity on a merchant ship or yacht, his flag is flown from the main masthead, or from a staff on the bow, if the ship has no mast.

The Union Flag is often referred to as the Union Jack, but it is only correct to call it the Union Jack when it is flying at the jackstaff of one of HM ships.

The Union Flag is not a recognised flag for a yacht to fly, and should never be flown by a foreign yachtsman as a courtesy flag. The correct flag for this purpose is the Red Ensign.

The Pilot Jack

This flag consists of the Union Flag with a white surround and may only be used by British Registered ships. It is very rarely used but, if desired, it may be flown from a jackstaff on the bow when in harbour or at anchor; it should only be flown when the yacht is wearing her Ensign, and it should be hoisted and lowered at the same time as colours are hoisted and lowered. The Pilot Jack is only flown at sea on dress ship days, i.e. when the yacht is at sea and dresses with mast head flags only.

Flag Q

This is specially noted in this part of the book because a yacht must, upon entering United Kingdom territorial waters, fly it to indicate to Customs that the yacht is arriving from foreign and requires clearance.

In the case of commercial ships Flag Q (or ZS under the 1969 International Code of Signals) means 'My vessel is healthy and I request free pratique'.

Other signals to indicate state of health are to be found in the International Code of Signals (1969).

The rules as to flying Flag Q when entering foreign territorial waters differ from country to country and the most up-to-date information will be found in cruising guides or the RYA books C1 and C2 *Planning a Foreign Cruise*.

The Diving Flag

Flag A from the International Code of Signals (1969) indicates 'I have a diver down; keep well clear at slow speed' and is the signal most generally used. Occasionally you may see NATO Flag No.4 (a white St. Andrew's cross with red background) or the USA Diving Flag (red

background, single diagonal white) in use. Rule 27(e) of the International Regulations for Preventing Collisions at Sea lays down a special rule for small craft in diving operations.

RACING FLAGS

As a general rule, although there are exceptions, no Ensign is worn when a yacht is racing. However, it may occasionally be necessary for yachts engaged, for example, in an offshore race, to *show their colours* when in foreign territorial waters or when entering a foreign port. On these occasions it is permissible for an Ensign to be worn although the yacht is racing.

As has been said before in this booklet, much of flag usage is etiquette, rather than law, and much has grown up by custom. In many yachting centres the wearing of an Ensign is sufficient to indicate that a yacht is not racing. The Ensign, removed at the preparatory (five minute) signal then indicates that the yacht is amenable to the Racing Rules.

It has for long been the custom that vessels, not engaged in racing, generally, as an act of courtesy, endeavour to keep clear of yachts that are racing.

It cannot now however, be anticipated that this will be the case. In any event, the rules of the road require specific action on the part of vessels meeting and it is now perhaps more likely than ever that vessels will stand on their rights according to those internationally recognised rules.

Retirement

If a yacht gives up or retires from a race the Ensign should be worn to show that the yacht is no longer amenable to the Racing Rules.

Protest

A protest flag is defined in the International Yacht Racing Rules, and is either Flag B of the International Code or a special flag as prescribed by the national authority of the country in which the club organising the racing is situated.

REFERENCE GUIDE FOR FLAG POSITIONING

	Motor Cruising Yacht	Single Mast Sailing Cruising Yacht	Racing Yacht
ENSIGN	Red unless entitled to wear a special Ensign. Worn from a staff at the stern.	Red unless entitled to wear a special Ensign. Worn from a staff at the stern.	Not whilst racing.
COURTESY ENSIGN	If *stub* mast has crosstrees then on starboard halyard.	Starboard crosstrees superior to all except Ensign.	N/A
CLUB BURGEE (On staff)	If no mast, from a staff on the bow or over a wheelhouse.	At masthead.	Not while racing. Rectangular flag if required by club offering racing.
FLAG OFFICER'S FLAG	Fly in preference to burgee of any other club, with associated Ensign.	At masthead superior to any other club burgee with associated Ensign.	Not while racing. Rectangular flag if required by club offering racing.
Q FLAG	If stub mast has crosstrees, on port halyard if courtesy Ensign is being worn.	Below courtesy Ensign if only one flag halyard. Otherwise on port halyard.	
HOUSE FLAG	On stub mast over wheelhouse. Not to be worn at sea.	Not to be worn at sea - if worn with courtesy Ensigns E & Q it should be inferior to both.	

UNION FLAG	The UNION FLAG should NEVER BE WORN AS A MARITIME ENSIGN OR COURTESY FLAG. It is used officially by certain high ranking Government Officers, worn from the mainmast head, or a staff on the bow. It is only called the UNION JACK when flown at the jackstaff of one of HM Ships.

REFERENCE GUIDE FOR FLAG POSITIONING

Racing Dayboat	Chartered Vessel	Yawl or Ketch	Gaff Rigged
Usually unable to wear one anyway; but not whilst racing.	Maritime flag (Ensign) of country to which yacht belongs.	Worn at a staff at the mizzen masthead if it cannot be worn at stern.	Peak of the sail on the aftermast if unable to wear at stern.
	Starboard crosstrees superior to all except Ensign.	Starboard crosstrees superior to all except Ensign.	Starboard crosstrees superior to all except Ensign.
Not whilst racing. Rectangular flag if required by club offering racing.	Burgee of charterer NOT OWNER.	From a staff at main masthead.	From a staff at main masthead.
Not whilst racing. Rectangular flag if required by club offering racing.	If charterer is a Flag Officer substitute for burgee.	Burgee or Flag Offiicer's flag from a staff at main masthead.	Burgee or Flag Officer's flag from a staff at main masthead.
	See Sailing Cruising Yacht.	See Sailing Cruising Yacht.	See Sailing Cruising Yacht.
	Though not a house flag, the courtesy Ensign of charterer's nationality may be worn at port halyard.		

POSITION AND IMPORTANCE OF HALYARDS

Signals on halyards are *read* in the following order:-
Starboard (outer): Port (outer): Starboard (inner): Port (inner).

PRIZE FLAGS

The custom of hoisting prize flags has virtually ceased but if it is desired to fly prize flags the following general comments may be of use:

The prize flag is a rectangular flag similar to a racing flag only smaller.

The second and third prizes are distinguished by the flag being hoisted inferior to the first prize. A blue flag marked with a white figure 2 signifies second prize, and a red flag marked with a white figure 3 signifies third prize.

The prize flags are flown on completion of racing to indicate any prizes won. The rules can be summarised as follows:

1. At the end of a day's racing, the prize flag is hoisted to indicate any prize won in the day's race.

2. At the end of a day's racing, when it is the last day of a regatta lasting several days, the yacht may hoist one prize flag for each prize won during that regatta, second and third prizes indicated by 2 and 3 pendants as already described. Alternatively, if the yacht is remaining in the port where the regatta was held, she may show all her prizes for that regatta on the day after the regatta ceases, e.g. on the Sunday. She may also show all prizes won in the regatta when she returns to her home port, flying the flags on arrival and the next day.

3. On the next day after the last race of the season a yacht can hoist prize flags showing all prizes won during the season, and she can also do this on return to her home port at the end of the season; generally, it is recommended that they be flown on the day after arrival as well. If the person in charge is confident that a prize has been won, the appropriate prize flag may be hoisted immediately after the end of the race.

If it is desired to fly from a yacht a series of prize flags to indicate prizes won in a regatta or over the season, these should be hoisted as soon as she anchors or moors after the last race of the series and, or in addition, they may be hoisted with the Colours in the morning.

When only a few prize flags are being flown they should be flown from the burgee halyards, below the burgee, or they may be flown from the starboard upper crosstrees.

When a large number of prize flags are flown, for instance at the end of the season, they should be flown on a dressing line from the main masthead to the taffrail or boom end, and if there are more flags to be flown than can be accommodated, the balance should be flown on a line from the masthead to the stem.

MOURNING

Mourning is indicated by wearing the Ensign and, in some cases, the burgee at *half mast*. The rules concerning the observance of mourning by yachts are as follows:

National mourning

This is observed on occasions such as the death of a member of the Royal Family.

Colours only, and not burgee, are half masted as soon as news is received and kept at half mast until sunset of that day, or, if the news is received during the hours of darkness, then the Colours are worn at half mast for the next day. Colours are again half masted during the time that the funeral is in progress.

The details vary considerably with the importance of the person in respect of whom the Colours are being worn at half mast. When any ships of the Royal Navy are present, owners are advised to ascertain the procedure they are using.

When the funeral of a naval officer or rating is in progress in a port where any of HM ships are lying, Ensigns and Jacks are half masted during the time the funeral is taking place. On these occasions, yachts present should follow the actions of HM ships.

A number of foreign countries have national days of mourning when Ensigns are worn at half mast; it is a courtesy for visiting yachts to conform with local practice.

Private mourning

If the owner of a yacht dies, the Colours and burgee should be half masted when the information is received and at sunset hauled down for the last time. Should the news be received during the hours of darkness, the Ensign and burgee should be worn and flown half mast next day, and finally hauled down at sunset on that day.

Should the death of a Flag Officer of a yacht club occur, there is no objection to yachts, which are lying in the home port of the yacht club and whose owners are members of the club, by mutual arrangement wearing their Ensigns at half mast for the same periods as are observed on the occasion of the death of the owner of a yacht.

Hoisting and lowering Ensigns and burgees on occasions when they are being worn at half mast

Ensigns and burgees should never be hoisted direct to or lowered from the half mast position. When being hoisted, they should first be hauled close up and then, after a pause of a few seconds, lowered to the dipped position. Similarly, when Colours or burgees are to be lowered, they should first be hauled from the dipped position close up and, after a pause of a few seconds, lowered. This is the correct ceremonial procedure.

SALUTES

It is customary for yachts to salute the following: All Royal Yachts; all warships, both British and foreign; Flag Officers of a yacht club when the yacht making the salute is wearing the burgee of that club. (It is customary when in their own waters for yachts to salute a Flag Officer only once a day.)

Salutes are made by dipping the Ensign, i.e. lowering it slowly to a position about one-third from the lower end of its hoist (the Ensign should not be lowered so far that it cannot fly). The ship making the salute keeps her Ensign at the *dip* until the ship being saluted starts to re-hoist her Ensign, when the ship making the salute re-hoists hers.

The burgee and the special flag of a Flag Officer of a yacht club should never be dipped when saluting.

Yachts entering or leaving a port, where the yacht club whose burgee the yacht is flying is situated, may salute the club by dipping the Ensign. This is more desirable if the flag of a Flag Officer is flying at the time from the club flagstaff. The club should respond by dipping its Ensign.

DRESSING SHIP
Dressing overall

This consists of stringing the flags of the International Code from the stem head to the masthead, from masthead to masthead (where the ship has more than one mast) and thence to the taffrail.

It is important that Ensigns, racing or other private flags should not be used on the dressing lines (i.e. the string of flags going overall), which should be confined to flags of the International Code of Signals. In arranging the flags on the dressing lines, triangular flags and pendants should, as far as possible, be placed between rectangular flags (this cannot be done throughout, however, as there are not enough pendants and triangular flags), and adjacent flags should be chosen to give as much contrast as possible, if the full complement of flags is unavailable.

All vessels should, as far as possible, be dressed alike. In general the order, reading from the bow, should be:

E, Q, p3, G, p8, Z, p4, W, p6, P, p1, I, Code, T, Y, B, X, 1st, H, 3rd, D, F, 2nd, U, A, O, M, R, p2, J, P0, N, p9, K, p7, V, p5, L, C, S.

In a single-masted vessel the line from bow to masthead could finish with 3rd substitute, and the line from masthead to stern carried on from D.

The line between masts in two-masted vessels starts with Y and finishes with O.

In addition to the ship's Colours (her Ensign) which should still be worn at its usual place, i.e. the Ensign staff on the taffrail, flags - generally Ensigns - should also be flown from each masthead when the ship is dressed. It is important that there is a flag at each masthead, and the flags flown at the masthead should be in accordance with the following:

1. For British national festivals British Ensigns are flown at all mastheads; at the main masthead the Ensign and the club burgee are flown side by side. There is, however, an exception to this rule when the owner of the yacht is a Flag Officer of a yacht club. In that case, his personal flag is flown by itself at the main masthead without any Ensign. It follows, that if such a yacht is a single-masted yacht, no masthead Ensign can be flown.

2. For foreign national festivals (either in British waters or abroad) an Ensign of the country in whose honour the ship is dressed is flown at the masthead. For schooners or yachts with more than two masts, the foreign Ensign is flown at the fore, for yawls and ketches at the mizzen, and for single-masted yachts it is flown at the main masthead alongside the club burgee. British Ensigns are flown at the other mastheads.

   As when celebrating British national festivals, the personal flag of a Flag Officer of a yacht club is always flown by itself at the main masthead. This produces a difficulty in the case of single-masted yachts and, under these circumstances, the foreign Ensign may be flown either at the starboard yard-arm or else at the crosstrees.

3. For local festivals, such as regattas, the club burgee should be flown at the main masthead with no Ensign. The owner's house flag may also be flown in its usual place or, alternatively, an Ensign may be flown. An Ensign should also be flown at all other mastheads where no other flag is flying.

In all the above cases, if the owner is entitled to wear the special Ensign of a privileged yacht club, he may fly either this Ensign at the masthead or a Red Ensign, but, should he elect to wear a special Ensign, the same special Ensign must be flown at the masthead. The special Ensign of one yacht club should never be flown from the masthead at the same time as the special Ensign of another yacht club is worn from the taffrail.

Dressing with masthead flags

When vessels are underway in the vicinity of an anchorage or are not fitted with dressing lines, they should hoist Ensigns at the masthead and Ensign staff and, where appropriate, they may also hoist the Pilot Jack at the jackstaff.

Dates for dressing ship

The principal national festivals of Great Britain currently celebrated by dressing ship are: Accession Day; Coronation Day; HM The Queen's Birthday; Commonwealth Day; HM The Queen's Official birthday (usually the first Saturday in June); HRH The Duke of Edinburgh's birthday.

In addition to these fixed days, ships are dressed on other occasions such as the marriage of a member of the Royal Family, the visit of Royalty to a port, etc. There should be no difficulty in ascertaining these dates, and yachts are advised to follow the action of ships of the Royal Navy when lying in a harbour where those ships are present.

Foreign countries have their own national festivals which are celebrated by dressing ship. Visiting yachts should, as a courtesy, follow the local customs.

It is customary to dress ship for a local festival.

RYA

MEMBERSHIP
Isn't it time you joined?

FOR THE FUTURE OF BOATING

RYA Isn't

The RYA is the national
organisation which represents the
interests of everyone who goes
boating for pleasure.

Personal membership is open to all
boat users.

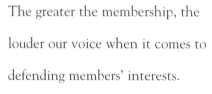

The greater the membership, the
louder our voice when it comes to
defending members' interests.

Make sure your voice is heard -
apply for membership today.

it time you joined?

Benefits of Membership include

- Access to expert advice on all aspects of boating from legal wrangles to training matters

- Special members' discounts on a range of products and services including boat insurance, books, videos and class certificates

- Free issue of certificates of competence, increasingly asked for by everyone from overseas governments to holiday companies, insurance underwriters to boat hirers

- Access to the wide range of RYA publications, including the quarterly magazine

- Third Party insurance for windsurfing members

Special Offers for RYA Members

- Free Internet Access with RYA-Online

- Discounts of up to 45% on a range of Yachting Magazine Subscriptions

- A Healthcare Cash Plan

- A privilege price structure for purchasing a Volvo car

- Plus regular offers in RYA Magazine

www.rya.org.uk

Membership application form

If you have previously been a member and know your membership number please enter here

[ ][ ][ ][ ][ ][ ][ ][ ][ ]

When completed, please send this form to:-
Royal Yachting Association RYA House Romsey Road Eastleigh Hampshire SO50 9YA

	Tick box	Cash/Chq.	DD
Family		£44	£41
Personal		£28	£25
Under 21		£11	£11

Please indicate your main boating interest by ticking one box only

W	SC	SR	PR	MC	PW	IW
☐	☐	☐	☐	☐	☐	☐

W = Windsurfing   SC = Sail Cruising   SR = Sail Racing
PR = Powerboat Racing   MC = Motor Cruising
PW = Personal Watercraft   IW = Inland Waterways

For details of Life Membership and paying over the phone by Credit/Debit card, please call 023 8062 7400

PLEASE USE BLOCK CAPITALS

	Title	Forename	Surname	Date of Birth	Male	Female
1.						
2.						
3.						
4.						

Address

Town   County   Postcode

Home Phone No.   Day Phone No.

Facsimile No.   Mobile No.

Email Address

Signature   Date

DISCOUNT IF YOU PAY BY DIRECT DEBIT - SEE ABOVE

Instructions to your Bank or Building Society to pay by Direct Debit

Please fill in the form and send to:
Royal Yachting Association RYA House Romsey Road Eastleigh Hampshire SO50 9YA Tel: 023 8062 7400

Name and full postal address of your Bank/Building Society

To The Manager   Bank/Building Society

Address

                Postcode

Name(s) of Account Holder(s)

Bank/Building Society account number

Branch Sort Code

Originator's Identification Number

9	5	5	2	1	3

Reference Number

Instruction to your Bank or Building Society
Please pay Royal Yachting Association Direct Debits from the account detailed in this instruction subject to the safeguards assured by The Direct Debit Guarantee. I understand that this instruction may remain with the Royal Yachting Association and, if so, details will be passed electronically to my Bank/Building Society.

Signature(s)

Date

Banks and Building Societies may not accept Direct Debit Instructions for some types of account

---

OR YOU CAN PAY BY CHEQUE

Source Code	Centre Stamp	Cheque enclosed	£	Made payable to the Royal Yachting Association	Office use only: Membership number allocated
077					

PART II YACHT SIGNALLING

Although radiotelephony is generally discussed in this booklet, the immense amount of necessary information regarding licensing and operating regulations, the choice of equipment, and how to use it including the handling of urgency, safety and distress traffic, forms the subject of other books from the RYA, in particular books G22 *VHF Radio inc GMDSS* and G26 *VHF Radio SRC Assessments*.

This book deals with visual signalling and signalling by sound when vessels are in close proximity as for example, in restricted visibility. The principal reasons for which a yachtsman needs to receive signals of one kind or another are:

1. To obtain weather forecasts and gale warnings.

2. To obtain time signals, more particularly when astro-navigation is used.

3. To obtain navigational information in various forms (e.g. from local port signal stations, lighthouses, light-vessels, Coastguards, and other ships or yachts).

4. To receive emergency signals from (or concerning) other craft.

5. To establish the nature of another vessel (e.g. during darkness or in fog) and to determine her movement relative to one's own ship.

6. To establish the identity (e.g. name, club and/or nationality) of another yacht or ship.

7. To receive messages for personal or business reasons, or messages which may affect the yacht's programme.

8. To be able to interpret signals used in connection with yacht racing (e.g. starting, cancellations, shortening courses, etc.).

There are perhaps fewer reasons for yachts being able to send signals, but they include:

1. The ability to send distress signals in as many of the accepted forms as possible and to pass other related information which is of help to would-be rescuers.

2. The ability to communicate regarding some other craft in distress, either with her or with another ship or shore.

3. To be able to pass important information (e.g. concerning safety or navigation) to another craft.

4. To be able to pass routine or personal messages as and when convenient (e.g. to notify people ashore of changes to the yacht's programme).

In order to meet these requirements various methods of signalling are available to yachtsmen. Some of them are relatively slow, but are simple and convenient over short distances and require little equipment or training. Others are more complicated and expensive, requiring more knowledge and experience.

The basis of many forms of marine communication is the International Code of Signals. The Code takes account of the wide and increasing use of plain language communications and it provides for all situations relating to safety of navigation and of persons, especially when language difficulties arise.

The International Code can be transmitted by any of the following methods:

1. Flag signalling, using the International Code flags. They consist of flags of different colours and shapes which are displayed in groups (or singly for the more important signals), and which can be interpreted from the code book, printed in nine languages. This method is rather slow, and it can only be used in daylight and in good visibility.

2. Flashing light, using the Morse Code. This code of dots and dashes is widely known and can be transmitted by light (day or night) over considerable distances—given a powerful light and good visibility.

3. Sound signalling, also using the Morse Code. Owing to the equipment used (e.g. whistle, siren or fog-horn) this method is slow. It can also cause confusion in poor visibility, when its use should be restricted to a minimum.

4. Voice over a loud hailer. Messages by loud hailer are normally passed in plain language, but the International Code may be used if there are language difficulties.

5. Radiotelephony – by voice over a marine radio. Messages are normally passed in plain language, but the International Code may be used in cases of language difficulties. Established procedures and licensing regulations must be followed. See RYA books G22 and G23 which explain these in great detail.

In addition to the above, sailors need to be familiar with other special or local signals which they will encounter. These include such items as combinations of shapes and flags (or lights by night) which control the entry to certain ports or indicate tidal heights, together with storm signals, distress signals, pilot signals, pratique messages, etc.

INTERNATIONAL CODE OF SIGNALS (1969)

Several signal codes for mariners were introduced in the early 1800's, perhaps the best known being Marryat's (1817) which can be fairly described as the first International Code. This used numeral flags 0 - 9, a *rendezvous* flag, a *telegraph* flag, a *numeral pendant*, two *distinguishing* pendants as *substitutes*, and the Union Flag. This code provided a total of 9,000 signals which was soon found to be insufficient, and in 1855 the British Board of Trade set up a committee to look into the problem.

As a result, a new International Code was introduced in 1857, based on the use of 18 flags, which were the consonants of the alphabet less X and Z. It was issued in two parts, the first part containing international signals and the second part only British ones. It was substantially revised in 1901 and again in 1943, on each occasion becoming more international in character. The more recent version (the 1931 International Code) was published in two volumes, one for visual and sound signalling and one for radio communications. It provided for seven languages - English, French, Italian, German, Japanese, Spanish and Norwegian. By means of the International Code, ships of these various nationalities could pass messages to each other without any knowledge of foreign languages at all. Apart from describing the actual flags, the meanings of the various groups, and the procedure for their use, it also detailed the methods of communicating by morse, semaphore and sound signals.

In the 1950's and 1960's a great deal of work by international committees (under what is now the International Maritime Organisation - IMO) resulted in a further revision of the Code, which was completed in 1964 and came into effect on 1 April 1969. Russian and Greek were added to the previous seven languages and all forms of marine communication combined into a single volume. As an example, all signals (including all the important single-letter signals) may now be made by any method of signalling, although there are restrictions on sound signalling to conform to Rules 34 and 35 of the Regulations for Preventing Collisions at Sea.

Each signal has a complete meaning. Signals consist of:

1. Single-letter signals, which are very urgent, important or common.

2. Two-letter signals for the General Section.

3. Three-letter signals beginning with M for the Medical Section.

In some cases *Complements* are used to supplement the available groups. Complements express:

1. Variations in the meaning of the basic signal, e.g.

CB = I require immediate assistance.

CB4 = I require immediate assistance. I am aground.

2. Questions concerning the same basic subject or basic signal, e.g.

DZ = Vessel (or aircraft) indicated appears to be in distress.

DZ1 = Is vessel (or aircraft) indicated in distress?

3. Answers to a question or request made by the basic signal, e.g.

IB = What damage have you received?

IB3 = I have not received any damage.

4. Supplementary, specific, or detailed information, e.g.

QL = You should go astern.

QL1 = You should go slow astern.

Complements which appear in the text more than once have been grouped in three tables, which are given on page 27. These tables should be used only as and when specified in the signal code.

In some groups, words appear in brackets. These are either alternatives, or information which may be included if it is available, or explanations of the text.

In the code itself, material is arranged under the following main headings: Distress, Emergency, Casualties, Damage, Meteorology, Communications, Pratique and Medical.

Cross references are given in the right-hand column, where appropriate, in order to facilitate coding.

General instructions

1. Numbers

Numbers are signalled as follows:

(i) Flag signalling: by the numeral pendants of the Code.

(ii) Flashing light or sound signalling: usually by numerals in the Morse Code, but may be spelt out in important cases (e.g. in giving a position).

(iii) Marine Radio or loud hailer: by the phonetic code words of the figure spelling table.

2. Decimal point

This is indicated as follows:

(i) Flag signalling: by inserting the Answering Pendant for the decimal point.

(ii) Flashing light or sound signalling: decimal signal AAA.

(iii) Voice: by use of the word decimal (pronounced DAY-SEE-MAL, as indicated in figure spelling table).

3. Depths

Should be signalled in feet or metres.

Figures followed by F = feet (*not* fathoms).

Figures followed by M = metres.

4. Azimuth or bearing

Signalled by three figures, denoting degrees from 000 to 359. Where necessary, to avoid confusion, the figures to be prefixed by A (for azimuth). Unless stated to the contrary, bearings are always signalled as True.

5. Course

As for azimuth, except that the figures are prefixed by C (for course).

6. Dates

Dates are signalled by two, four or six figures which are preceded by the letter D (for date).

The first two figures = day of the month. (When signalled alone they refer to the present month).

The next two figures = month of the year (e.g. D2012 = 20 December).

The final two figures, when six are signalled = year (e.g. D201201 = 20 December 2001).

7. Latitude

Signalled by four figures, preceded by L and followed by N for (North latitudes) or S (for South latitudes). N or S may be omitted where obvious. The first two figures indicate degrees and the second two indicate minutes.

8. Longitude

Signalled by four (or five) figures preceded by G and followed by E (for East) or W (for West). The last two figures indicate minutes and the first two (or three) indicate degrees.

9. Distance

Signalled by figures (in nautical miles) preceded by R.

10. Speed

Signalled by figures preceded by S (for knots) or by V (for kilometres per hour).

11. Time

Signalled by four figures, the first two denoting the hour (from 00 to 23) and the last two denoting minutes. When preceded by T the time indicated is local time. When preceded by Z the time indicated is Greenwich Mean Time.

12. Local signal codes

(when applicable) are preceded by the group YV 1 = The groups which follow are from the local code.

Morse code
Alphabet

A	• —
B	— • • •
C	— • — •
D	— • •
E	•
F	• • — •
G	— — •
H	• • • •
I	• •
J	• — — —
K	— • —
L	• — • •
M	— —
N	— •
O	— — —
P	• — — •
Q	— — • —
R	• — •
S	• • •
T	—
U	• • —
V	• • • —
W	• — —
X	— • • —
Y	— • — —
Z	— — • •

Numerals

1	• — — — —
2	• • — — —
3	• • • — —
4	• • • • —
5	• • • • •
6	— • • • •
7	— — • • •
8	— — — • •
9	— — — — •
0	— — — — —

Phonetic tables

Letter spelling table

Letter	Code Word	Pronunciation
A	Alfa	<u>AL</u> FAH
B	Bravo	<u>BRAH</u> VOH
C	Charlie	CHAR LEE
D	Delta	<u>DELL</u>TAH
E	Echo	<u>ECK</u> OH
F	Foxtrot	<u>FOKS</u> TROT
G	Golf	GOLF
H	Hotel	HOH <u>TELL</u>
I	India	<u>IN</u> DEE AH
J	Juliett	<u>JEW</u> LEE <u>ETT</u>
K	Kilo	<u>KEY</u> LOH
L	Lima	<u>LEE</u> MAH
M	Mike	MIKE
N	November	NO <u>VEM</u> BER
O	Oscar	<u>OSS</u> CAH
P	Papa	PAH <u>PAH</u>
Q	Quebec	KEH <u>BECK</u>
R	Romeo	<u>ROW</u> ME OH
S	Sierra	SEE <u>AIR</u> RAH
T	Tango	<u>TANG</u> GO
U	Uniform	<u>YOU</u> NEE FORM
V	Victor	<u>VIK</u> TAH
W	Whiskey	<u>WISS</u> KEY
X	X-ray	<u>ECKS</u> RAY
Y	Yankee	<u>YANG</u> KEY
Z	Zulu	<u>ZOO</u> LOO

Note
The syllables to be emphasised are underlined.

Figure spelling table

When numerals are transmitted by radiotelephone, the following rules for their pronunciation should be observed:

Numeral	Spoken as
1	WU N
2	TOO
3	TREE
4	FOW-ER
5	FIFE
6	SIX
7	SEV-EN
8	AIT
9	NIN-ER
0	ZERO
Decimal Point	DAY-SEE-MAL
Full Stop	STOP

Numerals should be transmitted digit by digit except that multiples of thousands may be spoken as such.

Procedure signals

Note
A bar over the letters of a signal means that the letters are joined together and made as one symbol.

1. Signals for voice transmissions (R/T or loud hailer)

Signal	Pronunciation	Meaning
INTERCO	IN-TER-CO	International Code group(s) follow(s).
CORRECTION	KOR-REK-SHUN	Cancel my last word or group. The correct word or group follows.

2. Signals for Morse transmission by light

$\overline{AA}$ $\overline{AA}$ $\overline{AA}$ etc.	Call for unknown station or general call.
$\overline{EEEEEE}$ etc.	Erase signal.
$\overline{AAA}$	Full stop or decimal point.
$\overline{TTTT}$ etc.	Answering signal.
T	Word or group received.

3. Signals for flags, radio-telephony and radio-telegraphy transmissions

CQ	Call for unknown station(s) or general call to all stations.

Note
When this signal is used in voice transmission, it should be pronounced in accordance with the letter spelling table (i.e. Charlie Quebec).

4. Signals for use where appropriate in all forms of transmission

AA   'All after . . .' (used after the 'Repeat' signal (RPT) - see below - means 'Repeat all after . . .').

AB   'All before . . .' (used after the 'Repeat' signal (RPT) - see below - means 'Repeat all before . . .').

$\overline{AR}$ Ending signal or end of transmission or signal.

$\overline{AS}$ Waiting signal or period.

BN   'All between . . . and . . .' (used after the 'Repeat' signal (RPT) - means 'Repeat all between . . . and . . .').

C   Affirmative - 'YES' or 'The significance of the previous group should be read in the affirmative'.

CS   'What is the name or identity signal of your vessel (or station)?'

DE   'From . . .'(used to precede the name or identity signal of the calling station).

K   'I wish to communicate with you' or 'Invitation to transmit'.

NO   Negative – 'NO' or 'The significance of the previous groups should be read in the negative'. When used in voice transmission the pronunciation should be 'No'.

OK   Acknowledging a correct repetition or 'It is correct'.

RQ   Interrogative, or 'The significance of the previous group should read as a question'.

R   'Received' or 'I have received your last signal'.

RPT   Repeat signal 'I repeat' or 'Repeat what you have sent' or 'Repeat what you have received'.

WA   'Word or group after . . .'(used after the 'Repeat' signal (RPT) means 'Repeat word or group after . . .').

WB   'Word or group before . . .' (used after the 'Repeat' signal (RPT) means 'Repeat word or group before . . .').

Notes

1. The procedure signals C, NO and RQ cannot be used in conjunction with single-letter signals.

2. Other signals relating to procedure are given under the heading of Communications in the International Code.

3. When these signals are used by voice transmission the letters should be pronounced in accordance with the letter-spelling table, except that NO is pronounced NO.

Single letter signals

The single letter signal may be made by any method of signalling. For those marked * see note (1) on next page.

A   'I have a diver down; keep well clear at slow speed'.

*B   'I am taking in, or discharging, or carrying dangerous goods'.

*C   'YES' ('Affirmative' or 'The significance of the previous group should be read in the affirmative').

*D   'Keep clear of me; I am manoeuvring with difficulty'.

*E   'I am altering my course to starboard'.

F   'I am disabled; communicate with me.'

G   'I require a pilot'. (When made by fishing vessels operating in close proximity on the fishing grounds it means 'I am hauling nets'.)

H   'I have a pilot on board'.

I   'I am altering my course to port'.

J   'I am on fire and have dangerous cargo on board; keep well clear of me'.

K   'I wish to communicate with you'.

L   'You should stop your vessel instantly'.

M   'My vessel is stopped and making no way through the water'.

N   NO ('Negative' or 'The significance of the previous group should be read in the negative'). This signal may be given only visually or by sound. For voice or radio transmission the signal should be NO.

O   'Man overboard'.

P *In harbour:*

'All persons should report on board as the vessel is about to proceed to sea'.

At sea:

May be used by fishing vessels to mean 'My nets have come fast upon an obstruction'.

Q 'My vessel is healthy and I request free pratique'.

*S 'I am operating astern propulsion'.

*T 'Keep clear of me; I am engaged in pair trawling'.

U 'You are running into danger'.

V 'I require assistance'.

W 'I require medical assistance'.

X 'Stop carrying out your intentions and watch for my signals'.

Y 'I am dragging my anchor'.

*Z 'I require a tug'. When made by fishing vessels operating in close proximity on the fishing grounds it means 'I am shooting nets'.

Notes

1. Signals of letters marked *, when made by sound, may only be made in compliance with the requirements of the International Regulations for Preventing Collisions at Sea, (Rules 34 and 35), accepting that sound signals G and Z may continue to be used by fishing vessels fishing in close proximity to other fishing vessels.

2. Signals K and S have special meanings as landing signals for small boats with crews or persons in distress.

The letter R has been omitted from the revised list of single letter meanings and a meaning has so far been unallocated, but see Rule 35(9) of the Collision Regulations.

Single letter signals with complements

(May be made by any method of signalling)

A with three numerals
= AZIMUTH or BEARING.

C with three numerals
= COURSE.

D with two, four or six numerals
= DATE.

G with four or five numerals
= LONGITUDE (the last two numerals denote minutes, and the rest degrees).

K with one numeral
= 'I wish to communicate with you by . ' (Complements table 1).

L with four numerals
= LATITUDE (the first two numerals denote degrees, and the rest minutes).

R - with one or more numerals
= DISTANCE in nautical miles.

S with one or more numerals
= SPEED in knots.

T with four numerals
= LOCAL TIME (24-hour clock).

V with one or more numerals
= SPEED in kilometres per hour.

Z with four numerals
= GMT (24 hour clock).

Tables of complements

Table I

1. Semaphore.
2. Morse signalling by hand flags or arms.
3. Loud hailer (or megaphone).
4. Morse signalling lamp.
5. Sound signals.
6. International Code flags.
7. Radiotelegraphy, 500kHz.
8. Radiotelephony, 2182kHz.
9. VHF Radiotelephony Channel 16.

Table II

0. Water.
1. Provisions.
2. Fuel.
3. Pumping equipment.
4. Fire ighting appliance.
5. Medical assistance.
6. Towing.
7. Survival craft.
8. Vessel to stand-by.
9. Ice breaker.

Table III

0. Direction unknown (or calm).
1. North-east.
2. East.
3. South-east.
4. South.
5. South-west.
6. West.
7. North-west.
8. North.
9. All directions (or confused or variable).

FLAG SIGNALLING

The flags used in the International Code (see inside front cover) remain as in the 1931 version of the Code and consist of:

1. Twenty six flags - one for each letter of the alphabet. These are all rectangular in shape, except A and B which are burgee shaped.

2. Eleven pendants - consisting of the 10 numerals 0-9, plus the Answering Pendant (or Code Flag as it is sometimes called).

3. Three triangular flags - the First, Second and Third Substitutes. These are used to avoid the necessity of a ship having to carry more than one set of the 26 flags and 11 pendants given above. They enable the same signal flag - either alphabetical flag or numeral pendant - to be repeated one or more times in the same group. Their use is described more fully below.

Definitions

Group

One or more continuous letters and/or numerals which together comprise a signal.

Hoist

One or more groups displayed from a single halliard. (Another use of the word *hoist* is to indicate the portion of a flag nearest to the line of the halliard - the *fly* being the other end which flutters in the wind.)

At the dip

A hoist or signal is *at the dip* when hoisted only about half-way up.

Close up

A signal is *close up* when it is fully hoisted, or when it is *two blocks*.

Tackline

A line used to separate the groups in a hoist, so that they are read separately.

Superior

A flag or group hoisted above another flag or group. (Note - flags are always read from the top downwards.)

Inferior

A flag or group hoisted below another flag or group.

Class

The class of a flag refers to whether it is an alphabetical flag or a numeral pendant. (See under the heading Substitutes).

Equipment required

In order to be able to signal using the International Code the following are necessary:

1. A complete set of the 40 flags. It should be emphasised that flags must be of an adequate size if they are to be identified at a worthwhile distance. 24in on the hoist by 30in on the fly is none too large for practical purposes. Yacht outfits are often smaller than this and of not much use except for dressing ship.

2. Flags must have a proper stowage, so that each is readily identifiable and can be quickly extracted. Large ships have flag lockers, but most yachts stow their flags in a canvas wallet which can be rolled up and put away when not required.

3. Bearing in mind the size of flags required, it is essential to have a halliard or halliards of sufficient length to make a hoist. While the height of mast should not present any problem in a sailing yacht, most of the stubby affairs fitted in modern motor yachts are useless for signalling.

4. A code book, with the meanings of the various groups.

5. Binoculars, in order to read signals from other ships.

Procedure

The basic procedure is that the sending ship hoists the identity (see under Identity of Vessels) of the ship she desires to signal. If the other ship's identity signal is not known she hoists the group VF ('You should hoist your identity signal') or CS ('What is the name or identity signal of your vessel (station)') - preferably at the same time hoisting her own identity signal. If the sending ship does not indicate the receiving ship by signal letters, then the signal is addressed to all ships within range.

The sending ship then hoists her signal, and when this is sighted the receiving ship hoists her Answering Pendant at the dip. When she has read the signal and is certain that she understands it she hoists the Answering Pendant close up.

The sending ship then lowers her signal - at which the receiving ship brings her Answering Pendant to the dip again. If the sending ship has a further hoist or hoists to make, the procedure is repeated, but if the message has been completed she hoists the Answering Pendant close up to signify End of Message. The receiving ship hoists her Answering Pendant close up to acknowledge, both then lower their Answering Pendants and the procedure is complete.

Identity of vessels

It is often necessary for ships and yachts to exchange their identities. The most obvious identification is a ship's nationality - by her Ensign. In addition all ships are allocated a registered number which actually consists of four alphabetical flags. For British ships the first is G or M. Registered yachts may apply for signal letters.

Signal letters are not compulsory for yachts, even if they are registered. When speaking to or calling a ship her signal letters precede the signal; when speaking of or indicating a ship they follow the signal.

Nowadays when ships meet on the high seas they often communicate by R/T or by light; the old procedure for *speaking* to a ship was to indicate:

1. National flag.
2. Signal letters.
3. Port from which sailed.
4. Destination.
5. Number of days out.
6. Longitude.

Substitutes

In order to provide for the repetition of one or more letters within a group, the Substitute flags are used. The First Substitute repeats the first flag of the group in the class which is immediately superior to it. Similarly the Second Substitute repeats the second flag in the group, and the Third Substitute the third flag. It must be remembered that *class* refers to whether it is an alphabetical or a numeral flag (see Definitions on page 28).

A substitute can only repeat a signal flag of the same class as that immediately preceding it. If a substitute follows one or more alphabetical flags, it repeats one of those flags; if it follows one or more numeral pendants it represents one of those pendants. The Answering Pendant when used as a decimal point should be disregarded when determining which substitute to use. No substitute can be used more than once in the same group.

The following are examples of the use of substitutes:

1. The signal BILL would be made by:
   B
   I
   L
   Third Substitute.

2. The group PPRP would be made by:
   P
   First Substitute
   R
   Second Substitute.

3. The signal T1330 would be made by:

T

1

3

Second Substitute

O

Note

Here two classes of flags are used, and the Second Substitute refers to the second numeral pendant - not to the second flag in the hoist.

Answering Pendant

The use of the Answering Pendant at the dip when a signal is first seen, and close up when it has been read and understood, has already been described under Procedure on page 29, also to signify 'End of Message' and to acknowledge same. In addition it is used to signal a decimal point between numeral pendants.

It may also be used by a Royal Navy ship while she is signalling with a non-naval ship or a shore station. Although the Royal Navy now uses International Code flags (supplemented by other naval numeral flags and other special flags and pendants), the International Code groups are not used between naval units. The answering pendant therefore indicates that a warship is using the International Code.

MORSE CODE BY FLASHING LIGHT

In order to pass messages satisfactorily it is necessary to have the right equipment; allthough over very short distances at night, almost any electric torch will suffice provided it is fitted with a suitable switch, but for greater ranges or for daylight signalling specialist equipment is used, e.g., an Aldis lamp. An Aldis lamp is essentially directional and must be kept trained on the receiving station using the sights provided - pressure on the trigger deflecting the reflecting mirror and forming the dots or dashes. This can naturally cause some difficulty in bad weather when, despite its shorter range, an all-round light (at the masthead for example) may be preferable.

Spacing

Morse is a matter of timing and rhythm. If a dot is taken as the unit of time, the following is the correct spacing, and this must be achieved if the message is to be clearly readable.

Dot	1 unit
Dash	3 units
Space between each dot or dash in a letter	1 unit
Space between each letter or symbol	3 units
Space between each word or group	7 units

The essential points to remember are that a dash is three times as long as a dot, and there must be a slight pause between each letter - otherwise EE would become 1, and AE would be read as R, for example. The pause between words is more pronounced, but this occurs almost automatically because (as will be seen below) the receiving ship or station acknowledges each word by making the letter T.

Procedure signals

The following procedure signals are used when sending and receiving Morse Code by flashing light. When a bar is placed on top of the sign the letters are run together without any pause between them.

Sign	Morse symbol	Meaning
A̅A̅ A̅A̅ A̅A̅ etc.	• — • — • — • —	Call up.
(until answered)	• — • — etc.	
T̅T̅T̅T̅T̅T̅ etc.		
(until call stops)	— — — — — — —	Answering signal.
T	—	Word received.
A̅A̅A̅	• — • — • —	Full stop or decimal point.
E̅E̅E̅E̅E̅E̅ etc.	• • • • • etc	Erase.

(Note: The five signals above are used only when sending Morse by light. The remaining procedure signals below can be used with other methods, as well as when using light.)

DE	— • • •	From.
RPT	• — • • — — • —	Repeat signal.
AA	• — • —	All after.
AB	• — — • • •	All before.
WA	• — — • —	Word or group after.
WB	• — — — • • •	Word or group before.
BN	— • • • — •	Word or group between.
A̅R	• — • — •	Message ends.
A̅S	• — • • •	Waiting signal or period signal.
C	— • — •	Affirmative YES.
R	• — •	Received.
YT4	— • — — — • • • • —	I cannot read your morse signalling lamp.
YU	— • — — • • —	Am going to communicate by International Code.

Morse procedure (flashing light)

The correct procedure for passing messages by flashing light is given in Chapter VI of the International Code. Briefly the transmitting ships are called up, either A̅A̅ A̅A̅ etc. or with the signal letters of the ship addressed, until answered. When ready to receive, the other ship makes the Answering Signal. If necessary the ships exchange identities, the transmitting ship making DE followed by her signal letters, which the receiving ship repeats back. The receiving ship then makes her signal letters, which the other repeats back.

Then follows the text of the message, either in plain language or in code groups (code groups being preceded by the signal YU). Each word or group is signalled separately and acknowledged by the receiving ship with the letter T. When proper names are to be inserted in code group messages and have been spelt out in plain language, they should be preceded by YZ (the words which follow are in plain language). At the end of the transmission the sending ship makes A̅R which the receiving ship acknowledges with R.

Notes on procedure signals

1. The General call signal (or call for unknown station) $\overline{AA}\ \overline{AA}\ \overline{AA}$ etc. is used to attract all stations in sight, or a station whose name or identity signal is not known. It is made until the Answering Signal is received.

2. The Answering Signal is made until the call up ceases.

3. The Erase Signal $\overline{EEEEEE}$ indicates that the last word or group was signalled incorrectly. It is answered by the Erase Signal. The transmitting station then repeats the message, commencing with the last word or group that was correctly signalled.

4. The Repeat Signal (RPT) is used by the transmitting station to indicate a repetition. If such repetition does not follow, the signal should be interpreted as a request for the receiving station to repeat back the signal received. It may also be used by the receiving station to request a repetition of the signal.

5. The Repetition Signals (AA, AB etc) are made by the receiving station after RPT to request repetition of the part of the signal indicated. For example:

   > RPT AA EP =
   > 'Repeat all after group EP'.
   >
   > RPT BN aircraft wreckage =
   > 'Repeat all between words aircraft and wreckage'.

   If a signal is not understood the Repeat Signal should not be used. In this case the group ZL ('Your signal has been received but not understood') would be appropriate.

6. The signal OK is used to acknowledge a correctly received repetition. The same signal is also used as an affirmative answer to a question, but normally the single letter C should be used to indicate an affirmative statement or an affirmative reply to an interrogative signal.

7. RQ converts a signal into a question. For example:

   > GZ = 'All persons saved'.
   > GZ RQ = 'Are all persons saved?'

8. For a negative reply to a question, or for a negative statement, the signal N is used in visual signalling (and NO is used for voice communication).

9. The signals C, N (or NO) and RQ cannot be used in conjunction with single-letter signals.

10. Waiting Signal AS is used either between groups as necessary to separate them (to avoid confusion) or after the end of a signal to indicate that the other station should wait for a further transmission.

Transmitting morse

The inexperienced signalman who makes and receives morse quite slowly will find it best to err on the side of making dots rather shorter than the prescribed proportion of three dots to one dash. That is to say the difference should be made more distinct, otherwise it is sometimes difficult to appreciate their relative lengths, because the dots and dashes do not follow each other very quickly.

Learning the morse code

Over the years various methods of learning morse have evolved. You can start by mastering the letters composed only of dots (E,I,S and H) and only of dashes (T,M and O); then there are the opposites, K (_._) and R (._.), P (._ _ .) and X (_.._). Two dots first for F (.._.) and two dots last for L (._..) help to distinguish between these two. No doubt many signalmen subconsciously remember Q (_ _._) by 'Here comes the Queen' (the short word 'the' corresponding to the position of the dot).

It does not make any difference whether the code is learned or practised by working with a light or with a buzzer. Using a light you can familiarise yourself with the code flashing into a mirror - a suitable hand torch will do. If you have a tape recorder you can prepare your own buzzer lesson on tape. Another instructional aid is a set of cards on each of which is a letter of the alphabet on one side, and the equivalent morse symbol on the other.

With two people the problem is simplified, since they can make random letters to each other in order to learn the code, and eventually pass complete messages backwards and forwards, using the correct procedures.

Throughout, it is most important to maintain the correct spacing of dots, dashes and pauses, and also to regulate the speed of sending so that a gradual improvement is maintained.

Morse code by other methods

Although morse code by flashing light is the method most likely to be used by yachtsmen, the following methods are also available:

1. Radiotelegraphy. For yachtsmen this is normally restricted to identifying the alphabetical call signs of any remaining marine radio beacons. The transmission of morse by buzzer over radio (or line) telegraphy used to be used extensively. However it is no longer used in this way.

2. Sound Signals. Morse Code can be transmitted by sound signals using the ship's foghorn, whistle or siren. This method is restricted to urgent or important signals and is described in Sound Signals below.

SOUND SIGNALS

Sound signals in restricted visibility

The requirement for ships to make sound signals in fog, mist, heavy rain or other conditions restricting normal visibility (whether by day or night) are in Rule 35 of the International Regulations for Preventing Collisions at Sea (1972). The full text, annotated for yachtsmen, is contained in RYA book G2, and should be studied carefully.

By Rule 33, a vessel of 12 metres or more in length shall be provided with a whistle and a bell and a vessel of 100 metres or more in length shall, in addition, be provided with a gong.

A vessel less than 12 metres is not obliged to carry the signalling appliances above described but if she does not she must have other means of making an efficient sound signal.

Sound signals in restricted visibility are as follows:

Power vessel making way through water
A prolonged blast at intervals of not more than 2 minutes.

Power vessel under way but stopped (i.e. not at anchor)
Two prolonged blasts at intervals of not more than 2 minutes.

Vessel at anchor
Ring the bell rapidly for about 5 seconds, at intervals of not more than 1 minute.

Vessels over 100m at anchor
In addition to above, sound gong aft at similar intervals.

(In addition, a vessel at anchor may sound R on her foghorn to warn an approaching vessel).

Vessel towed
One long blast followed by three short, every two minutes.

Vessel aground
As for at anchor, plus three separate and distinct strokes of bell before and after.

Pilot vessel on duty
Four short blasts

Vessel under sail, or not under command, or constrained by her draught, or engaged fishing or towing
One long followed by two short blasts, at least every two in minutes.

Hence in fog or restricted visibility a sailing vessel will sound one long followed by two short blasts at intervals of not more than 2 minutes but if she is less than 12 metres she shall not be obliged to give the above-mentioned signals. She must, however, have other means of making an efficient sound signal.

The provision of an efficient foghorn on a small yacht is something of a problem. The best proposition is a hand-operated pump in a sailing yacht. Horns blown by mouth or aerosols are ineffective under most conditions. Motor yachts can and should be equipped with a proper horn.

Vessels in sight of each other

Rule 34 prescribes signals for power-driven vessels in sight of each other as follows:

One short blast
> I am altering course to starboard.

Two short blasts
> I am altering course to port.

Three short blasts
> I am operating astern propulsion.

When either of two vessels approaching each other fails to understand the actions or intention of the other, or is doubtful that sufficient action is being taken to avoid a collision, she shall give at least five short and rapid blasts.

The whistle signals above may be supplemented by an all-round white light, with the number of flashes equivalent to the number of blasts.

In a narrow channel, when overtaking can only occur if the overtaken vessel takes action to permit safe passing, a vessel intending to overtake shall indicate her intention by the following whistle signals:

Two long blasts followed by one short
> I intend to overtake you on your starboard side.

Two long blasts followed by two short
> I intend to overtake you on your port side.

If in agreement the overtaken vessel sounds one long, one short, one long and one short blast, and takes the necessary steps. If in doubt she may sound five or more short and rapid blasts.

Sound signals for distress purposes

Under Annex IV the following constitute distress signals, and should not be used for any other purpose:

1. A gun or other explosive signal fired at intervals of about a minute.
2. The continuous sounding of any fog-signalling apparatus.

Urgent and important signals

The International Code makes special provision for sound signalling, using the ship's whistle, siren or foghorn. Since the misuse of these signals could cause serious confusion, the method is normally confined to urgent and important signals. The system is necessarily slow. Sound signalling in fog should be reduced to a minimum. Signals other than the single-letter signals below should be used only in extreme emergency (when no other means of communication is available), and never in frequented waters.

The following letters, when made by sound, may only be used as in Rules 34 and 35 of the Collision Regulations.

E, I and S	Manoeuvring and Warning Signals - Rule 34.
B,D,H & T	In restricted visibility - Rule 35.
B	For a vessel being towed - Rule 35(e).
D	For a vessel not under command, or sailing, fishing or towing - Rule 35(c).
H	For a pilot vessel on pilotage duty - Rule 35(j).
T	For a power driven vessel under way - Rule 35(a).

Sound signals - procedure

No call or answering sign is made for the single-letter signals mentioned previously, and identities are not exchanged. No special procedures are given for other sound signals, transmitted by ship's siren, whistle, foghorn, etc. The signals shown in Clause 4 of Procedure Signals may be used as appropriate. It should be remembered that single letter signals marked by asterisks may only be made by sound in compliance with the International Regulations for Preventing Collisions at Sea. In general the sending ship simply makes her message, ending with AR, the receiving ship then makes her message, ending with AR, the receiving ship then making R to signify that she has received the signal. Signals should be made slowly and clearly;

they may be repeated, if necessary, but at sufficiently long intervals to ensure that confusion does not arise. The receiving ship can make the Repeat Sign (RPT) if she misses a word.

Warning signal

Under Rule 34 (e), a power-driven vessel is required to sound one prolonged blast as a warning when approaching a bend in a river or channel where a vessel coming in the other direction cannot be seen.

DISTRESS SIGNALS - GENERAL

Of all the signals which a yachtsman may have to send or read in a hurry, possibly without reference to any book such as this, distress signals are the most important. Under conditions when a yacht is in real danger there is no time to consult the signal book. In the same way, distress signals should be recognised instantly.

Every owner and skipper should make sure that his boat carries adequate distress equipment and signals, depending on her size and type, and on the waters in which she sails. It is important that all on board should know where distress and emergency equipment is stowed and how to use it.

Methods of indicating distress include:

- The distress warning signal on GMDSS radio followed by a plain voice MAYDAY message. For more information see RYA books G22 and G26

- For non GMDSS radios the spoken word MAYDAY on marine radio followed by a plain voice MAYDAY message.

- Signals transmitted by EPIRBs and SARTs

- Red parachute flares fired one at a time at short intervals or red pinpoint hand held flares.

- Orange smoke signals, for use in daylight. These consist of a buoyant container, which after ignition is thrown into the sea and generates smoke for about 2-3 minutes.

Hand flares are satisfactory for smaller boats and are efficient at ranges of up to 5 miles. Most makes available to yachtsmen burn for almost a minute with a candlepower of 15,000. Parachute flares are the best option for distress signalling at night, since they operate for almost a minute at a height of over 300m. Under good conditions they can be seen for 20 miles or more by night, and 5 miles by day. While they are admittedly considerably more expensive than hand flares, they are much more effective. Most of these pyrotechnics have a limited life and therefore need to be renewed periodically in accordance with the maker's instructions—normally about every three years. Flares should be stored in watertight containers.

- The letters SOS in morse, by light or any other signalling method.

- The International Code Flag signal NC.

- The continuous sounding of any fog signalling apparatus (e.g. foghorn, siren or whistle). In order to avoid any possible doubt as to the intention of the signals, the continuous sounding should be made in the form of a succession of letters SOS.

- A gun or other explosive signal, sounded at intervals of about a minute. (This signal is normally not suitable for small craft, but yachtsmen should be aware of its significance).

- A square flag (or something resembling a flag), with a round object either above or below it.

- Flames, from burning rags soaked in paraffin or oil (not a particularly effective signal, and rather a last resort).

- Raising and lowering the outstretched arms slowly.

It must be strongly emphasised that the use of any of the above signals, except for distress purposes, is forbidden. Even then they should only be made with the authority of the skipper, and only in cases of serious and imminent danger requiring urgent assistance, or on behalf of another ship in such danger which, for some reason, cannot itself make a distress signal.

Replies to distress signals

The following signals from ashore indicate that a ship's distress signals have been received and that assistance will be given as soon as possible:

By day

An orange smoke signal, or combined light and sound signal - three single signals fired at intervals of about 1 minute.

By night

A white star rocket, consisting of three single signals fired at intervals of about 1 minute.

Landing signals for boats with rescued persons

Meaning - 'This is the best place to land.'

By day

Vertical motion of the arms or of a white flag.

Green star signal.

International Code signal K by light or sound signal.

By night

Vertical motion of white light or flare.

Green star signal.

International Code signal K by light or sound signal.

Meaning - 'Landing here is highly dangerous.'

By day

Horizontal motion of a white flag, or arms extended horizontally.

Red star signal.

International Code signal S by light or sound signal.

By night

Horizontal motion of white light or flare.

Red star signal.

International Code signal S by light or sound signal.

Where landing is signalled as dangerous, a more favourable landing place may be indicated as follows:

1. By placing or carrying another white flag, or light, or flare in the direction to be indicated.

2. By firing a red flare vertically and a white star in the direction towards the better landing place.

3. By using the code letter S, followed by R if the landing is to the right, or L if it is to the left of the approach line.

Signals used by aircraft on search and rescue operations

The following signals may be used by aircraft to direct ships towards another ship, or aircraft, in distress:

1. In sequence, the aircraft first circles the ship at least once. It then crosses low, close ahead of the ship, opening and closing the throttle, or changing the propeller pitch. Finally, it heads in the direction in which the ship is to be directed. The signal may be repeated.

   The aircraft is directing the ship towards the ship or aircraft in distress.

2. The aircraft passes close astern of the ship, at low altitude, opening and closing the throttle, or changing the propeller pitch.

   Indicates that the assistance of the ship is no longer required.

MISCELLANEOUS SIGNALS

There are a variety of signals at sea which are applicable to special situations. Some of these such as Pratique Messages (or Quarantine Signals) are of direct interest to yachtsmen. Others are unlikely to be used in, or may not be applicable to, small private vessels; nevertheless the yacht skipper should at least be aware of their existence and know where to find the details if required.

Pratique messages

All yachts, whether carrying dutiable stores or not, arriving in the United Kingdom from outside the EU - including the Channel Islands - must fly Flag Q. Details are given in Customs Notice No. 8, which can be obtained from any Customs

House or from HM Customs and Excise website: www.hmce.gov.uk

Pilot signal

The following signals relate to pilotage and it is an offence, under the Pilotage Act (1913), to use them incorrectly, or for example to fail to show the correct signal in waters, where pilotage is compulsory.

Meaning - 'I require a pilot' (which can be signalled by any method)

By Day or Night
International Code Signal G

Under International Regulations for Preventing Collisions at Sea (1972), Rule 35, *a power-driven pilot vessel when engaged on pilotage duty may, in addition to the signals prescribed in subsections (a), (b) or (9), sound an identity signal consisting of four short blasts.*

Fishery protection ships and fishing vessels

A code of signals exists, and is internationally agreed, for communication between fishing vessels and Fishery Protection Ships. The code makes use of Ensigns and coloured flags, but is not of direct interest to yachtsmen.

Port signals

British Ports. Local signals control entry to (and departure from) certain ports and harbours around the coasts of the British Isles. These signals are detailed in the appropriate Admiralty Pilot, to which reference should be made.

In addition, the Ministry of Defence might, in certain circumstances, control the entry to special ports and institute an Examination Service for vessels which approach them. In such cases, where entry is prohibited, this is indicated by three red balls disposed vertically by day and three all-round red flashing lights disposed vertically by night.

International port traffic signals

This system is still in an introductory stage, but its use is bound to spread.

The rules for this system are:

1. The main movement message comprises three lights disposed vertically and no additional light may be added to this column. Hence three vertical lights indicate a traffic signal, and not lights of navigational significance.

2. Red lights mean 'Do not proceed.'

3. Green lights mean' 'Proceed, subject to the conditions stipulated.'

   It should be noted that, to avoid confusion, red and green lights are never shown together.

4. A single yellow light, shown to the left of the column carrying main messages Nos 2 or 5, at the level of the upper light, means ' Vessels which can safely navigate outside the main channel need not comply with the main message'. This is obviously significant to yachtsmen.

5. Signals which are auxiliary to the main message may be adopted by local authorities. Such signals should use only white and/or yellow lights, and be displayed to the right of the column carrying the main message.

It can be seen that the basic signals are fairly easy to memorise. Ports with complex entrances and much traffic need various auxiliary signals, which need to be documented. Small harbours need only two or three of the basic signals.

Some signals may be omni-directional - shown to all vessels simultaneously. Others must be directional - shown to vessels either entering or leaving, but not both.

Signal number five assumes that some other means of communication such as VHF radio, signal lamp, loud hailer, or auxiliary signal is used to inform the vessel that she may proceed.

Number one signal, for a serious emergency, must be flashing lights. All other signals must be either fixed or slow occulting lights (the latter being useful when background lights are a problem). A mixture of fixed and occulting lights must not be used.

Tide signals

At certain ports, signals are displayed (normally by a combination of various shapes by day, and of lights by night) to indicate the height of the tide, or the depth of water at the entrance, or over the bar.

Reference should be made to local sailing directions or the appropriate Admiralty Pilot since, particularly in the United Kingdom, a variety of different signals are in use.

International port traffic signals - examples

No	Lights		Main message
1	R R R	Flashing	Serious emergency - all vessels to stop or divert according to instructions.
2	R R R	Fixed or slow occulting	Vessels shall not proceed.
3	G G G		Vessels may proceed. One way traffic.
4	G G W		Vessels may proceed. Two way traffic.
5	G W G		A vessel may proceed only when she has received specific orders to do so.
			Exemption signals and messages
2a	Y R R R	Fixed or slow occulting	Vessels shall not proceed, except that vessels which navigate outside the main channel need not comply with the main message.
5a	Y G W G		A vessel may proceed only when she has received specific orders to do so, except that vessels which navigate outside the main channel need not comply with the main message.

APPENDIX

International Code - selected groups

AC	I am abandoning my vessel.
AE	I must abandon my vessel.
AF	I do not intend to abandon my vessel.
AN	I need a doctor.
CB	I require immediate assistance.
CB 4	I require immediate assistance. I am aground.
CB 5	I require immediate assistance. I am drifting.
CB 6	I require immediate assistance. I am on fire.
CB 7	I require immediate assistance. I have sprung a leak.
CJ	Do you require assistance?
CK	Assistance is not (or is no longer) required by me (or vessel indicated) .
CV	I am unable to give assistance.
DX	I am sinking.
ED	Your distress signals are understood.
EF	SOS/MAYDAY has been cancelled.
FA	Will you give me my position
IL	I can only proceed at slow speed.
IM	I request to be escorted until further notice.
IT	I am on fire.
IZ	Fire has been extinguished.
JG	I am aground. I am in a dangerous situation.
JH	I am aground. I am not in danger.
JI	Are you aground?
JL	You are running the risk of going aground.
JO	I am afloat.
JW	I have sprung a leak.
JX	Leak is gaining rapidly.
KM	I can take you in tow.
KN	I cannot take you in tow.
KQ	Prepare to be taken in tow.
KR	All is ready for towing.
LG	You should prepare to cast off towing hawsers.
LO	I am not in my correct position. (To be used by a light vessel).
MG	You should steer course . . .
NC	I am in distress and require immediate assistance.
NG	You are in a dangerous position.

NH	You are clear of all dangers.
PD	Your navigation light(s) is (are) not visible.
PH	You should steer as indicated.
PI	You should maintain your present course.
PP	Keep well clear of me.
QO	You should not come alongside.
QP	I will come alongside.
QR	I cannot come alongside.
QT	You should not anchor. You are going to foul my anchor.
RA	My anchor is foul.
RB	I am dragging my anchor.
RN	My engines are out of action.
SC	I am under way.
SD	I am not ready to get under way.
SQ	You should stop or heave to.
UM	The harbour or port is closed to traffic.
UN	You may enter harbour immediately.
UO	You must not enter harbour.
UW	I wish you a pleasant voyage.
VJ	Gale is expected from direction indicated. } Complements
VK	Storm is expected from direction indicated. } Table 111.
YT	I cannot read your . . . Complement Table 1.
YU	I am going to communicate with your station by International Code.
YV	The groups which follow are from the International Code of Signals.
ZK	I cannot distinguish your signal.
ZL	Your signal has been received but not understood.
ZM	You should send (or speak) more slowly.
ZD 2	Please report me to Lloyd's London.